To those who come from nowhere...

Caen, my town, was once famous for its cobbled streets, its evil-smelling courtyards, its historic buildings - and its fine minds. But a storm laid waste to all that in 1944. Caen, thirty years on, has acquired a new face, the appearance of a modern town with an ability to limit its expansion to what is reasonable, show off its past glories to their best advantage, and provide for its population a lifestyle that is the envy of many.

For those who only pass through the town, Caen often comes as a complete surprise for it has not yet imposed its new image and it remains largely unknown. Yet visitors to Caen like to spend time in the town, learning something of its history ; they enjoy being taken for a stroll for just a few hours. These few lines will help tourists to make the most of their visit ; even better, they may then be encouraged to stay for a while or even come back at a later date.

It is vital to be able to put down family roots in a town, to feel part of the unbroken line of generations through the ages who also sought happiness in this same place. It is essential to feel like the branch of an age-old tree rather than an isolated blade of grass that will disappear with the passing of summer. The sense of belonging to a group, of being interdependent across the years, is the best antidote to the rampant anxiety of our times. This is why

this booklet, which was written as a guidebook for tourists passing through the town, is also dedicated to all the people of Caen, many of whom have settled here only recently and still have much to learn about their town.

Man may be one of the rare beings to have the power of changing his environment, but he is also influenced by it. This is why it is so important that towns should be beautiful and stimulating, and not just functional. The buildings that bear witness to the past have their own part to play, a dynamic and contemporary role rather than a mere illustration of a history that is long gone.

When you are born in a town and when, at the age of twenty, you see it die slowly, day after day, beneath the bombs, you feel ties with it that are rooted in the very depths of your being. When later on, you have an opportunity to take part in its development and help, in your own small way, to give it back its soul... you fall in love with it and you feel as if this love is something that must be shared. More than a guide, this book is intended to help readers discover the heart of Caen, the heart that is still beating today, the heart that has already been beating for centuries, and which will continue to beat for many a long year, for the joy of those who live there and know how to listen to it. Caen, my town, the town I love and that you are sure to fall in love with too.

The past : the origins of the town

Just as a beautiful woman never reveals where she comes from, Caen's origins are shrouded in mystery. At the dawn of our era, man had already settled here. The most recent archaeological digs have shown that, in Gallo-Roman times, a ''vicus'' or fairly extensive village existed near the Monastery. This may have been the Roman Cadomum, or Gallic Catomagos which gave us the name Caen. It seems to have died out towards the end of the 3rd century, probably after invasion by the

barbarians. Later, there was a village on St. Martin Hill - the remains of a church and a 7th-century graveyard were uncovered at the end of the Rue de l'Académie.

At periods as yet undefined, other small villages came into being - Darnetal (in the St.Peter district), Calix, and Vaucelles. In 1025, a text mentions Cadomus which was by then no more than a string of scattered villages surrounded by fields and marshland.

Behind St. Peter's Church is the **Leroy Tower**, a remnant of the town walls which were breached at this point by the ''Petite Orne'' river.

Frank Duncombe

The Story of Caen

Photographs by Philippe Thomas

Translated by Angela Moyon

ouest france

The Anglo-Norman period

William the Conqueror (1027-1087) made Caen his capital, and commissioned the building of the castle, the Monastery (Abbaye-aux-Hommes), and the Convent (Abbaye-aux-Dames). He also gave impetus to the spread of its influence by turning the scattered villages into a real town. The ramparts on the castle and the town centre, the Bourg le Duc, date from 1060 ; remains can be seen near the old St. Stephen's Church and on the Fossés Saint-Julien (St.Julian Moat). The Bourg-l'Abbé and Bourg-l'Abbesse grew up around the abbeys but were not fortified until 1356. The conquest of England (1066) linked the town to the kingdom across the sea for several centuries and confirmed its position as a large town with a maritime bias. The town was connected to the sea by the R. Orne, with its various tributaries, the Odons and the Noë. The Monastery was reached by boat in those days. What we now know as the Boulevard Leclerc was a waterway in which the chevet of St.Peter's Church was reflected until last century... Caen, the Venice of Normandy, was perhaps more poetic in those days but it was also more evil-smelling and more unhealthy.

It was John Lackland who, in 1203, raised Caen to a borough, governed by a mayor selected from three names proposed by the upper middle classes. Soon, though, the King had to flee the continent and, in 1204, the town opened its gates to Philip Augustus.

Although a French town, its destiny continued to be marked by the English throughout the One Hundred Years' War.

After landing in Saint-Vaast-la-Hougue in 1346, the English troops captured Caen and, to punish the population for its resistance, ransacked it, and subjected it to pillaging and arson. For years, anarchy reigned in the region, until Du Guesclin (whose statue stands on the Fossés Saint-Julien) arrived in Caen in 1373 and put an end to the "hoards of bandits". In 1417, King Henry V of England landed in Touques and besieged Caen. Despite the fortifications, and the resistance of garrison and population alike, the town fell after more than six weeks of very bitter fighting. Again, it was subjected to pillaging and murder. Several thousands of people died, and more than half the population emigrated.

The English then wanted to turn Caen into their own town, despite regional resistance, some of it armed. It was in 1432 that the University was founded with the Faculty of Law first then, in 1436, the Faculty of Arts and Theology and, in 1438, the Faculty of Medecine. But in 1450, the English were defeated in Formigny near Arromanches and they left Normandy. The One Hundred Years' War was drawing to a close, Richemont and Dunois captured Caen and, on 6th July, King Charles VII of France entered the town as its liberator.

Life under the French

A century of peace enabled Caen to expand and increase its wealth again through the royal factories, trading activities and shipping in its harbour. These were the days of the Renaissance, which have bequeathed to us the chancel of St. Peter's, the Than, Mondrainville and Escoville Mansions and the Men-at-Arms' Manorhouse.

The 16th century was marked by the Wars

of Religion and the ransacking of the local churches by the Protestants in 1562 remains an unforgettable event in the town's history, with the mass destruction of statues, the profaning of William the Conqueror's tomb etc. The Black Death of 1584 is another major event. It killed nearly 10,000 people and unfortunately returned on several occasions.

In 1588, after Rouen had joined the Lea-

(Top) :
Old St. Stephen's beside the ramparts. Its nave now lies in ruins.
(Bottom) :
St. John's in the heart of the "island" that bears the same name. It was never completed because the foundations were unstable, as shown by the crooked porch. The entire lower town, which was built on a former marsh, was still subject to flooding until recent times.

guers, Henri III transferred Normandy's high judicial court to Caen, where it remained for a few years. In that same year, the "Salvador", one of the ships in the mighty Spanish Armada sent to attack England, foundered on the rocks off the coast, which were then given its name. Over the years, the word was deformed until it became Calvados and, during the French Revolution, the name was given to the entire *département*. It was also in the 16th century that the town's fortifications were completed, thereby creating a new urban district - the Place Royale (now the place de la République). Peace returned when Henri IV mounted the throne and, in 1594, he created a new free-trade fair. It still exists to this very day and opens on the second Sunday after Easter, but it has undergone major changes over the centuries.

In 1620, there was yet another insurrection when the castle garrison, which had given its support to Marie de Medici, took up arms against the town that was traditionally loyal to the sovereign, at that time Louis XIII. The king came in person to re-establish law and order. The castle narrowly missed being razed to the ground but luckily wisdom prevailed. In 1624, 1626, and 1631, the plague again took its toll of the population. The 17th century was marked by the founding of a number of convents, the construction of private mansions on the Ile Saint-Jean (which was completely flattened in 1944), and the setting up of the Caen Academy "a source of the sharpest wits". These were the days of the foundation by Father Eudes of the Order and seminary that bear his name. Thanks to the unstinting efforts of Prior Dom Baillehache, they were also the days of the restoration of St. Stephen's Basilica which had been ruined by the Wars of Religion.

With the early 18th century came the rebuilding of the Monastery by monks from the Congregation of St. Maur who gave it the form we see today. Some of the urban districts were also opened up when the town's fortifications were demolished. The same period saw the building of the Place Saint-Sauveur and the Place Fontette, named after the Intendant who commissioned the work.

During the French Revolution, Caen supported the federalist ideas of the Girondin faction. In punishment, the keep in the castle built by Henri I Beauclerc, William the Conqueror's son, was razed to the ground. It was from Caen that Charlotte Corday set out in 1793 to assassinate Marat, symbolising the determination of the local people and their utter dislike of any form of excess.

The second half of the 19th century was a time of expansion - construction of the canal linking Caen to the sea (it was opened in 1850), laying-out of the St. Peter Basin (where the Saint-Gilles meadows had once lain) in 1848, the covering of the rivers Odon, the doubling of the number of bridges over the Orne, and the arrival of the railway in Caen itself (the station was almost built on the Prairie). This was also a time of major intellectual influence and one name merits a particular mention - Arcisse de Caumont, the father of modern archaeology.

With the dawn of the 20th century came the first metalworks on the outskirts of Caen - the Société Métallurgique de Normandie, and a number of shipyards, all of which gave the town a whole new appearance. Until the outbreak of the Second World War, the town continued to undergo balanced expansion (Saint-Louis district) and began to spread into the suburbs on both banks of the Orne. Major urban development projects were undertaken, e.g. the improvement of sanitation (1930), and the removal of the famous cobblestones. Then came ...

6th June 1944

By dawn the thunder of cannonfire along the coast could already be heard, and the continuous passage of aircraft and British radio stations informed the local people that the Allied landings had taken place on our beaches. At 1 p.m. the first air raid hit the centre of the town. At 4 p.m. there was a second raid, at 10 p.m. there was a third one and, at

St. Peter's has always stood in the centre of the town and today it still holds a special place in the hearts of the people of Caen. Its Renaissance chevet used to be mirrored in the river, now the setting for the flower market.

2.40 a.m. on the morning of June 7th, the whole of the town centre was flattened and set ablaze by the bombing. The population sought refuge in the Monastery ; the town had been born here and would surely not be allowed to die. Its church also took in the refugees, as did the Good Saviour which was housing the only temporary hospital still intact. More than 5,000 people took shelter in an area marked out by huge red crosses and indicated to the Allies by the Resistance Movement. The Allies were close to the town but it took them another month to enter it. From the rooftops, the fighting could be seen on the plains round about.

Life was gradually re-organised among the ruins despite continuing bombing raids. On 12th June, a mortar shell demolished the bell-tower of St. Peter's. Some of the population sought refuge in the quarries at Fleury, but more than 15,000 people remained in the town by choice or because they were unable to leave. There were thousands of people killed or injured. Everything had to be improvised. Much is owed to the members of the civil defence force, the teams of emergency helpers and the Red Cross who cooperated in the effort. On 7th July, 1,000 low-flying bombers flattened the ruins and whatever had been left standing - the town hall, the Place de la République and the university, and the Rue Pasteur all went up in flames.

Finally, on 9th July, the British and Canadian troops entered Caen, guided by the Resistance which hoisted the first French flag in Caen that evening in front of St. Stephen's, but they were grave-faced and had suffered too much to show any joy. The right bank had still not been liberated. From then on, it was German mortarfire that rained down on the town. The "Battle of Caen" was to last more than two months and 75 % of the town was destroyed. From the station to the castle, and from the St. Peter Basin to the Prairie, there were ruins as far as the eye could see.

Reconstruction

Mr. Brillaud de Laujardière, Chief Architect, drew up the plans for a new town, clearing the areas round historic buildings, widening roads, giving the town a unity that was well-suited to its history by making use of stone and slate. There was a general regrouping of property and those who had lost their homes were grouped in cooperatives. The town was divided into blocks and entrusted to the architects and builders once the rubble had been cleared. Because of the type of soil, nearly all the buildings had to be constructed on piles. The area around the castle was cleared, the university was resited although the stubborness of its Rector, Mr. Daure, made sure that it remained within Caen. Anything that was not a vital part of the town centre was rebuilt on the outskirts. For years, then, the town was one vast building site in which life was gradually beginning to return to normal. It took 25 years to rebuild the community. It had lost the wonderful buildings that bore witness to its history, but was more beautiful than before and ready for a new phase of expansion similar to the periods of development experienced in past centuries.

Expansion

While the rebuilding work was going on, the town was beginning to expand and new districts were springing up in the countryside on the outskirts of the old town e.g. La Guérinière, La Grâce de Dieu, le Calvaire Saint-Pierre, Venoix, and la Pierre-Heuzé. Industrial expansion continued with the arrival of several new factories - Radiotechnique, Saviem, Citroen to name but the largest. The industrial estates in Mont-Coco, Mondeville and Le Canal were being equiped with all necessary amenities. Caen then enjoyed one of the largest growth rates in France. Its position as regional capital was confirmed in many different fields, as was its importance with regard to the tertiary sector. It was already a taste of things to come.

St. Peter's. The ambulatory around the chancel of St. Peter's is particularly ornate.

Caen today : a few statistics

Population :
125,000 inhabitants : ranks 27th among French towns.
53,000 inhabitants are less than 21 years old. There is a working population of 40,000, half of them employed in the tertiary sector.
These figures can be compared with the populations in 1936 (60,000) and 1946 (50,000).

Administrative function :
Regional capital of Lower Normandy.
County town of Calvados.

Transport :
140 miles from Paris by motorway.
1 hour 50 minutes from Paris by turbotrain (10 trains a day).
Airport in Carpiquet.
10th-largest port in France linked to the sea by the canal. Caen is twinned with Würzburg (W.Germany) and is involved in Calvados' twinning with Devon (Great Britain).

Education :
More than 40,000 pupils in over 100 schools and colleges.
University : 12,000 students, 17 different teaching and research units (law, arts, science, medecine, and pharmacy).

Sports :
9 stadiums ; 37 gymnasia and sports halls.
Sports Centre seating 3,500 spectators.
3 swimming pools, 1 skating rink.

Culture :
Drama : Atelier Lyrique. Comédie de Caen (National Drama Centre). Théâtre du Gros Caillou (children's theatre).
National Academy of Music (1,500 students).
Caen Chamber Orchestra.
Arts and experimental cinemas.
Art Gallery.
Normandy Museum (ethnography).
Municipal library.
Regional Art School.
8 youth and arts centres.

Social services :
Teaching hospital.
Cancer treatment centre.
Psychiatric hospital.
6 surgical clinics.
5 old people's homes.
4 nurseries.

Environment :
300 hectares of parks and gardens (20 sq. meters per inhabitant).
25,000 trees in the town.
A 500-hectare municipal forest 9 miles south of the town.
The coast 9 miles to the north : environmental and leisure centre.

The surrounding area :
D-Day Beaches, Arromanches Museum.
Lisieux and the Auge Region.
Bayeux and Queen Matilda's tapestry.
The "Norman Alps".
Deauville.

A walk round the town : The Place Saint-Pierre (No.1 on the map)

We start our stroll on the Place Saint-Pierre, the centre of the town. For centuries, this has been the heart of the community. The very first town hall, the "Chatelet", was built on the bridge of the same name that crossed the Petite Orne or Noë. The river has been canalised and now flows beneath the Boulevard Leclerc. Thereafter, between 1754 and 1792, local dignitaires settled in :

The Escoville Mansion on the square, now the Tourist Information Office. Its façade, which lost much of its complexity when it was rebuilt after the 1944 bombing raids, is of less interest than its inner courtyard. Go inside for a moment and you will find a fine example of Italianate Renaissance architecture. Built between 1533 and 1540 for a rich merchant named Levallois d'Escoville, the mansion

Quatrans House. Built in the 14th century for Jean de Quatrans, this is one of the few half-timbered houses still standing in the town.

dates from the same period as the chevet of St. Peter's Cathedral and was designed by the same architect. Note the statues of Judith holding Holofernes' head and David holding Goliath's head. The mansion was purchased in 1652 by Moisant de Brieu who founded the Academy of Caen. Its head office is still here. Now the property of the town council, the Escoville Mansion is used for exhibitions and meetings.

Behind St.Peter's Church is the **Leroy Tower,** the remains of the ramparts which were broken up at the foot of this tower by the Petite Orne river.

St. Peter's Church (église Saint-Pierre) was built between the 13th and 16th centuries over foundations that were much older (pre-Romanesque). It had an eventful history, the most memorable dates being 1562 when the Huguenots destroyed the statues, stained glass windows and furnishings, and 1944 when the belltower collapsed after a direct hit by a mortar shell from the British battleship ''H.M.S. Rodney''. It has been rebuilt exactly as before. The French Revolution also left its mark. The building became a Temple of Reason, which is decidedly odd given the marked lack of Classicism in its architecture. The nave is Gothic and the 234-foot tower, which is a wonder in the same style, never fails to astonish visitors for its soaring airiness. It owes this to the colonettes supporting the octagonal spire decorated with star tracery and the impression is further heightened by the bell turrets at the corners. The chevet is especially remarkable for its wealth of ornamentation. It was designed by Sohier and is a Renaissance masterpiece, with bell turrets and carvings that are very unusual in this part of the world. Rather than entering the church (unless you are particularly fond of its gilded 18th-century High Altar), walk down to the Rue de Geôle from which the view of the doorway and rose window, both of them topped by openwork pediments, is made all the more unusual by the fact that the tower stands slightly off-centre. A little further on is the :

Quatrans House, built in the 14th century for Jean de Quatrans, a barrister in Caen. This is one of the few timbered houses still standing in Caen. Only the front is timbered ; the remainder is built of stone, which is more understandable in our town. It houses the offices of the Regional French Buildings Conservation Department.

The castle (No. 2 on the map)

Most of the older people in Caen saw the castle as it really was for the first time after the bombing raids of 1944. Before that, it was totally hemmed in by houses, some of which adjoined the ramparts, and the Army had built barracks in it. Showing the castle's 5 hectares to their best advantage has been one of the success stories of the town planners involved in the rebuilding of the town. William the Conqueror had the first ramparts built (half-a-mile long), with his castle inside. His son, Henri Beauclerc, continued the work, and had the keep and Exchequer built. Philip Augustus strengthened it and had the moats dug. Although the citadel has capitulated on more than one occasion, it has never been captured. Restoration projects and digs undertaken since the last war make this an interesting place to visit.

The Town Gate (Porte de la Ville) is preceded by a barbican built by the English in 1440. Beyond it is **St. George's Chapel,** once the parish church for there were numerous houses within the castle walls (as well as several churches). The building, which dates mainly from the 15th century, has some 12th-century features. Today, as a memorial to the ''Battle of Caen'', an unknown victim of the bombing raids has been laid to rest there.

Further along, on the left-hand side, is the **King's Manorhouse** or ''Governor's Residence'' (it was intended for him) built in the 17th and 18th centuries. It houses the Nor-

(Top) :
The chancel of St. Peter's is decorated with a veritable piece of lacework in stone.
(Bottom) :
The cloisters in the Monastery (Abbaye-aux-Hommes). The building now houses the town hall.

mandy Museum (traditional arts and crafts, archaeology, ethnography).

On the north side is the **Exchequer,** a marvel of Romanesque vernacular architecture, now used for receptions. It was an integral part of the palace, whose sub-foundations can be seen close by, and was the ceremonial hall. The Exchequer of Normandy (or Ducal Court) met there but this was not its only purpose. It got its name from the checkered cloth covering the table. It was originally divided in two by a wooden floor, but underwent numerous modifications and was used successively as an army storehouse, stables and a ruin lived in by local tramps. It finally regained the dignity more befitting its title as the ancestor of the British Parliament and the name that it gave to Her Gracious Majesty's Ministry of Finance.

Beside the palace sub-foundations, digs uncovered the remains of the **keep,** one of the largest in France but unfortunately demolished in 1793 on the orders of the Convention. This was punishment for having imprisoned members of the Convention in it when they were sent to put down the intrigues fomented by the Girondin federalists who had sought refuge in Caen. It was one of these parliamentarians, Romme, who devised the poetic Republican calendar during his term of imprisonment here.

Further north are the admirable buildings of the **university,** standing on 33 hectares of ground (although this is only half the total area of the campus). After passing the 14th-century Porte des Champs (Field Gate), your walk will take you back down into the town. On your way, you will see the **Art Gallery,** a modern building that blends in well with its surroundings. Like the Normandy Museum, this gallery is well worth a visit.

The **Normandy Museum,** founded in 1963 and housed in the Governor's Residence, has collections of traditional, domestic, agricultural and craft items from the Normandy of days long gone, as well as reminders of popular art in times past.

The **Art Gallery** (Musée des Beaux-Arts) is a modern building housing collections first put together in the days of the First Empire - Tintoretto, Veronese, Rubens, Van Dyck, to mention but the oldest of the artists. Their works are hung near a collection of 19th-century canvases by Courbet, Delacroix, Monet etc. In addition, the gallery holds the Mancel Collection of fifty thousand engravings by Dürer, Rembrandt, Callot, and the famous **Madonna and Child** by Van der Weyden.

N.B. : Both the museum and art gallery are closed on Tuesdays.

Before leaving the castle, take a walk round the walls. You will be able to see down the new Avenue du 6-Juin to the south and across the old Bourg-le-Roi to the west with its various belltowers. In the distance to the east is the squat outline of the **Convent** commissioned by Matilda, William the Conqueror's wife, and her final resting place. Although it underwent major restoration during the last century, it is nevertheless worth a visit for its Romanesque nave, its chancel full of carved capitals and, more than all else, its crypt which is a veritable forest of stone.

Nearer the castle is the **Sepulchre,** now a cultural centre, at the other end of the picturesque Vaugueux district. The building dates from the 16th century and stands on the site of a collegiate church that was destroyed during the Wars of Religion. It was built to the same design as the Church of the Holy Sepulchre.

Guardroom. It was here that the remains of the earlier town of Caen were discovered. In the 13th century, the monks built the Guardroom here and it was used for important secular or religious meetings. Now the setting for regional and civic assemblies, the building bears witness to the town's long existence. Its name, the Guardroom, remains an anachronism.

(Overleaf) :
The castle, founded by William the Conqueror, was completed by his son, Henri Beauclerc. The towers along the ramparts are more recent and the barbican dates from the time of the English occupation. The houses that once huddled round it were cleared after the 1944 air raids and the castle now dominates the town centre. It contains the Art Gallery, the Normandy Museum and the Exchequer.

The town

Cross the pedestrian precinct and the Place Saint-Pierre again and you will find yourself at the **Than Mansion,** a beautiful 16th-century building that has undergone major restoration. The Rue Hamon leads you to the Rue Saint-Pierre where there are two half-timbered houses serving as reminders of the Caen of old. And here you are at St. Saviour's (Saint-Sauveur) or, to be more precise, in Notre-Dame de Froide-Rue.

The Rue Froide (No. 3 on the map)

As you cross the tiny square, note the statue of Malherbe.

The church of **Notre-Dame de Froide-Rue** is immediately striking because of its two adjacent aisles. The older of the two (14th century), on the garden side, was given an apse during the Renaissance but originally dated from the same period as the belltower that once stood outside it. Although the tower is less grandiose than the one that tops St. Peter's, it may well have been used as a model, for the two are very similar. In the 15th century, the aisle running alongside the Rue Froide was added, beyond the belltower. It has a strange outside staircase which now leads nowhere.

The **Rue Froide** is one of the few streets in Caen to have maintained its original appearance and it has been shown off to its full advantage by the relaying of the road in the old style. It is a pedestrian street in which you can wander at will to see the shops (many of them antique shops) that have been restored beneath the arcades. From the inner courtyards, you can see some attractive dormer windows and old staircases. No. 16, in the Sens yard, has been a printer's since the 17th century and is one of the district's particular traditions. On the wall opposite the church is a detailed description of the houses.

Place Saint-Sauveur (no. 4 on the map)

At the end of the street, turn left into the Place Saint-Sauveur, laid out in the 18th century on the orders of the Intendant, Fontette, at the same time as the square beyond it which bears his name. The late 17th-century law courts have never inspired archaeologists. On the other hand, the square itself has some fine mansions, in particular no. 20 built in a pure Baroque style and recently restored. In the centre of the square is a statue of Louis XIV in the guise of a Roman emperor ! Originally erected on the Place Royale to replace the one that had been destroyed during the French Revolution, it was resited in front of the Monastery in 1883, and it was not until after the war that it finally arrived here, in a much more appropriate setting. Until the early 19th century, this was the site of the pillory used for executions and public torture.

St. Saviour's Church (église Saint-Sauveur) is now a ruin and has not yet been restored. The belltower has a Romanesque base but the nave dates from the 15th century. It suffered many misfortunes. In the 18th century, it was given an inelegant porch. During the Revolution, the church fell into disuse and became the Butter Market, which it still is. Its steeple was demolished in the last century, for economic reasons. It is to be hoped that the building soon regains more dignity.

This is the site of the traditional Friday-morning market, reminding the locals that their town was first and foremost a place of trade with the rich countryside round about. From there, you can either go directly to the Town Hall or take :

On all sides of the **Place Saint-Sauveur,** there are fine mansions, all of which have been restored. On Friday mornings, a picturesque market is held on the square, the descendent of the Monday market that took place here before the days of William the Conqueror. Although cattle trading has now ceased, the market is still filled with local produce sold by smallholders from the outlying rural areas.

A detour via Notre-Dame (no. 5 on the map)

Go down the **Rue des Fromages** (named after a family that once lived there), another pedestrian precinct. It was once nicknamed the Rue Monte-à-Regret (Climbed-with-regret Street) for it led to the pillory! Turn left into the Rue Ecuyère (one of the few streets left intact in Caen) and you will reach a small square where the Beautiful Cross once stood. This was the final stop for condemned prisoners. Malherbe's birthplace (he was born in 1555) is a later building on the site of the original. It stands opposite the Rue Saint-Laurent that leads to :

Notre-Dame de la Gloriette. The parvis is closed off by chains that stopped traffic entering the street where the university once had its premises so that the students were not disturbed during lectures! Notre-Dame (also known as "La Gloriette") is the former chapel of the Jesuit monastery founded in 1684 in the Pré-des-Esbats, at a time when this area of meadowland jutting out into the heart of the town was being "developed". Built in a pure Jesuit Italianate style, it was given a huge decorated altar after the Revolution. The altar was dated 1707 and came from the Convent. The church was placed at the disposal of the town council a few years ago and, once it has been restored, it is to be used as a concert hall as it seemed predestined to be ; its original name was Sainte-Catherine-des-Arts.

We are now on the former **Place Royale** (now Place de la République !), which dates from the early 18th century. Modern gardens cover an underground car park. Note the Daumesnil Mansion beside the post office. The square, whose sides were once all the same length, was closed off at one end by the monastery of the Fathers of the Mission, or Eudists. During the French Revolution, the monastery was turned into the town hall, and it remained so until 1944. It was flattened during one of the last air raids. On the ground, a fragment of the foundations of the old chapel is still visible.

Pass the County Buildings (Préfecture) that were extended during the First Empire and contain some fine reception rooms dating from that period. Pass the post office inaugurated before the war by President Albert Lebrun, and go down the **Boulevard Bertrand** that runs along an oxbow lake formed by the Odon rivers. Behind the wall on the right-hand side is the fine front of the Gosselin de Manneville Mansion (1760), the residence of the region's Prefect. As you reach the square, look to your right - the Regional House is all that remains of the famous **Mount College** created in the 15th century in the residence of the abbots of Mont Saint-Michel, and a forerunner of today's high school. In the 17th century, it was taken back by the Jesuit Order (Notre-Dame church is just behind it).

Old St. Stephen's (No.6 on the map)

Probably built on the site of the oldest church in Caen, St. Stephen's (le vieux Saint-Etienne) has been destroyed on several occasions and again suffered major damage in 1944. The building dates from the 14th century with later additions. Note the huge Flamboyant Gothic stained glass window, with a headless statue of a horseman beside it. The statue was wrongly thought to represent William the Conqueror ; it is now thought to be Emperor Constantine! The church fell into disuse during the French Revolution and was

used as a storehouse for the roads department. It is now an archaeological museum housing the collection of the Antiquaires de Normandie, an association founded by Arcisse de Caumont (the street bears his name). Behind the church are the remains of the 9th-century fortifications of the "old town".

There is a great difference between the levels of church and square, a reminder that Caen grew out of scattered villages. The "old town" which included old St. Stephen's Church was crisscrossed by arms of the R.

Old St. Stephen's (Vieux St. Etienne) is one of the oldest churches in the town. It stands adjacent to the ramparts and was often badly damaged over the centuries. Today, it houses an archaeological museum with the collection put together by the Société des Antiquaires de Normandie founded by Arcisse de Caumont.

Odon, one of which flowed through what is now the grounds of the County Buildings. Another ran along the course of the Boulevard Bertrand (named after the Mayor who had the river filled in). The old town was surrounded by ramparts and it is part of these walls that stands almost touching St. Stephen's. There was no access from here to the Monastery surrounded by the walls of Bourg-l'Abbé. A large section of these walls stands opposite the municipal library. When the remainder was demolished, the level of the roadway was raised. The fine layout of the square is a recent innovation and it, too, has a story attached to it. The layout decided upon when the Espla-nade de l'Hôtel-de-Ville was opened up meant that the County Buildings had to lose part of its grounds. But the County Offices did not see eye to eye with the Mayor of the day and refused to part with the land. It was not until a few years later that the quarrel died down and the road could be given a more rational layout.

As you cross the square, you can see the 15th-century belltower of St. Nicholas' in the distance behind St. Stephen's. The church would be worth a visit for the pure Romanesque lines of the nave and chancel, but at present it is not open to the public.

The Monastery (no. 7 on the map)

Our walk then takes us to the Esplanade Jean-Marie Louvel (ex-Mayor of Caen, died in 1970). The gardens, relaid in accordance with 18th-century designs, is filled with shrubs and plants that flower in successive seasons of the year, providing a perfect setting for one of the finest town halls in France. To the right and left are buildings erected last century for the grammar school; opposite, at the end of the square, is the new central library (the second largest in France). And facing the library is a section of the Bourg-l'Abbé ramparts.

William the Conqueror commissioned the Monastery (Abbaye-aux-Hommes) on the site of older buildings. The church, which was begun in 1066, was dedicated to St. Stephen. Lanfranc was its first Abbot before becoming Archbishop of Canterbury. All that remain of these 11th-century buildings are the nave and towers on the church; the chancel and spires date from the 13th century. The central lantern tower replaced an earlier 390-foot belltower that collapsed in 1566. The church was ruined in 1562, during the Wars of Religion, and almost lost its chancel as a result. This section of the building was restored in 1626, thanks to the stubborness of the Prior, Dom Jean de Baillehache. The monastery buildings were entirely rebuilt from 1704 onwards, using plans drawn by a monk named Guillaume de la Tremblaye, but they were never finished because of the French Revolution.

Napoleon set up the Imperial Grammar School there and so it remained until 1965 when the town council turned it into the Community Centre.

The main entrance stands in the centre of the 340-foot façade of the east wing. On the left is the **calefactory,** the monks' reading and leisure room, now used for municipal exhibitions; on the right is the **chapter house,** the setting for Caen's civil weddings. It contains some wonderful Louis-XV style oak panelling that is reminiscent of the woodwork in Versailles. It also houses huge paintings purchased from a Jesuit convent in Paris in 1764 - Bourdon's ''Crossing of the Red Sea'' and ''Moses striking the rock'' by Mignard. In the sacristy behind the chapter house, which also has wood panelling, there is a painting by Lebrun, ''Moses killing an Egyptian''. The main staircase in the foyer is an admirable piece of work, seemingly suspended in mid-air, and its wrought iron handrail and the grille in the corridor on the first floor are masterpieces of iron work. The first thing that strikes visitors entering the 97-foot long **refectory,** now used for receptions, is the Louis XV woodpanelling. At the end of the room is a painting by Lépicié called ''William landing in England'' (but he is dressed as a Roman warrior!). In the medallions are Restout's ''Pilgrims on the road to Emmaüs'', and the landscapes above the door are charming.

The monastery (Abbaye-aux-Hommes). Its West front dates from the beginning of the Norman Romanesque period and is the architype of what was later to become a harmonic Norman façade, i.e. with the towers and central doorway at the end of the nave all on the same line.

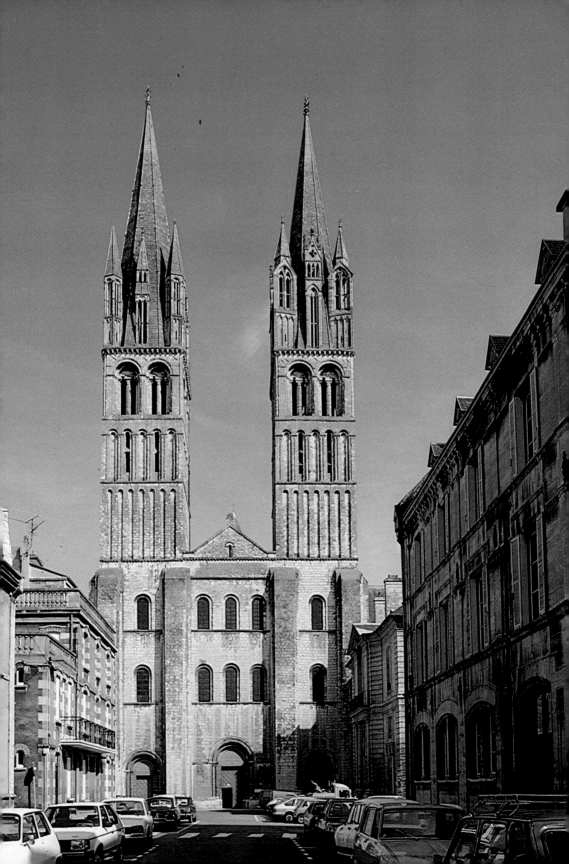

On the south side of the courtyard is the splendid **guardroom,** which is well worth a visit. Built in the late 12th century, it was used as a ceremonial hall and the Exchequer of Normandy met there. It is now used for regional and municipal meetings, having recently undergone major restoration work because during the First Empire it was completely disfigured to accommodate some of the grammar school classes. In particular, the floor on the upper storey has been laid with ceramic tiles that are reminiscent of the original floor covering.

From the Classical **cloisters** on the north side, there is a fine veiw of the nave and towers. Foundations of large Gallo-Roman buildings were uncovered in the garth and under the floor of the guardroom.

The **parlour** is a fine oval room with wood panelling, a foretaste of the Louis XVI style. It has a strange modern slabbed floor designed to divide the room into ten equal parts. From the windows, there is a view of the **King's palace,** a 12th-century building that was restored from top to bottom in the 19th century. It was used to accommodate visiting sovereigns and VIP's. It has been purchased fairly recently by the town council and now houses the town's archives.

Leave the monastery by what was once the visitors' entrance, on the **Place Monseigneur-des-Hameaux.** A monument was erected here in memory of a brief visit to Caen by the Duke de Berry in 1814. It was here, on 9th July 1944, that the first French flag to fly over Caen again was hoisted, after the town had been liberated.

The West front of St. Stephen's Minster is strikingly plain. It dates from the beginning of the Norman Romanesque period when its design was considered as something entirely new. The 260-foot spires are from a later period and are a foretaste of the Gothic style. The Romanesque nave is impressive for its height and its austerity. In the chancel is the tomb of the Duke-King, rebuilt in the early 17th century having been pillaged by the Pro-

testants. Later it was again pillaged, this time by the Revolutionaries, and today it contains only one of his bones. The man to whom Caen owes its position as a major city was destined to be refused the tranquillity of a proper grave. In fact, he almost had no grave at all because one of the local people objected to the burial on the grounds that he had never been paid for the land on which the church stood. He interrupted the funeral service by making a hue and cry. Even in those days, the Normans had fully acquired the notion of property and a sense of what was owing! The organ, which was restored by Cavaillé-Coll, is one of the finest Romantic instruments anywhere and is used for magnificent concerts.

Within the town hall are two interesting collections :

— the **Museum of Norman Costume** based on a legacy from Madame Messager containing authentically old pieces of clothing e.g. head-dresses, scarfs, dresses and costumes.

— a **Museum of Basic Nature Skills,** housed in a former bakery behind the guardroom. Slide shows and audiovisual programmes showing stuffed animals provide information on the main species of bird and mammal living in Normandy.

Contact the town hall, Service des Affaires Culturelles.

Caen's coat-of-arms is a gold crenelated tower and keep on a red background, and is probably based on the crest of the Viscounts of Caen. Some people believe that the tower represents the original town hall (the Châtelet on St. Peter's Bridge), while the red background is the colour of the Dukes of Normandy. The first known example of the coat-of-arms dates from 1439. During the course of its history Caen, which was known as the ''good town'' because of its loyalty to the king, had the right to include fleur-de-lys in its emblem. Today, it has regained its original coat-of-arms, flanked by the decorations received by the town which was made a Che-

Top :
The Exchequer. Standing within the castle grounds, this is a wonderful example of vernacular Romanesque architecture.
Bottom :
The reception room in the town hall was originally the **monks' refectory.** The late 18th-century oak panelling has been remarkably well-preserved.

valier of the Legion of Honour on 2nd June 1948. It is also the holder of the Croix de Guerre with bar and the Medal of the Resistance Movement.

The remainder of the visit (by car)

From the town hall, head for **"La Prairie"**, a vast open space in the heart of the town and one of its main features. It is frequently flooded in winter, when it turns into a lake. A right granted originally by the Dukes of Normandy enabled the inhabitants of Caen and a few neighbouring villages to acquire the second crop of grass, after payment of a tax to the "Maréchal de Venoix". It was this custom that saved the Prairie from being included in building projects on a number of occasions. Now it belongs almost entirely to the town council and it has a preservation order on it. Since 1837, it has been used for horse-racing. These days, the meetings held at this modern track remind the local people that their town lies in the very heart of a region famous for breeding the very best French trotters.

Leave the Prairie by way of the war memorial and head for the **Place de la Résistance**, a wonderful example of the successful reconstruction of the town centre. The statue of Joan of Arc, brought back from Oran, reminds passers-by that Caen became a new home for many families who were forced to leave Algeria.

The area round **St. John's Church** (église Saint-Jean) was cleared after the air raids and the 14th- and 15th-century building can now be admired in its entirety. Both towers have remained unfinished because of risks of subsidence. In fact, the doorway is slightly crooked although this was corrected during the initial building work. The church as a whole is said to stand on oak piles.

The Rue des Carmes takes us to the **St. Peter Basin.** Caen harbour used to stretch from here to the chevet of St. Peter's Church but it was gradually covered over and the present basin, which dates from the 19th century, is used for shipments of timber. A marina is also being laid out. As for the harbour, it is constantly expanding and now stretches from Caen to Ouistreham, between the R. Orne and the canal.

From here, we climb up to St-Gilles. **Holy Trinity Church** got its name from the old church of which only one doorway remains, opposite the newer building. It was built with the convent founded by William's wife, Matilda, who is buried there. This remarkable Romanesque construction used to be topped with spires but they were destroyed in the 14th century. There is a majestic nave. Note the Byzantine decoration and the crypt, a veritable forest of stone. The convent buildings, rebuilt in the 18th century to plans by Guillaume de Tremblaye (who was also responsible for rebuilding in the Monastery) used to house a hospital before being turned into an old people's home. They are now used as offices, by the regional cultural services.

Let us now return towards the **University,** rebuilt to plans by H. Bernard, and situated on a vast 32-hectare campus that is already too small. The Phoenix of Leygues symbolises the rebirth of this dynamic institution that is nevertheless of venerable age, for it was founded in 1432 by the English. Opposite the University, to the left, is a small patch of woodland. This is the old Protestant cemetery containing the grave of the famous dandy, George Brummell, who ended his tumultuous life in Caen. Occasionally, a few flowers laid on his grave show that he still has faithful admirers, even in our very materialistic century.

After passing the "Gaillon" and the Rue Bosnières, we reach the **Park** (Jardin des Plantes) founded in the 18th century to grow medicinal plants. In addition to them, it now has several wonderful botanic collections, both outside and in the greenhouses. It is also a little corner of nature in the centre of the town and is much appreciated by the local people.

A few steps lead to **St. Julian's,** a modern oval-shaped church that combines concrete and glass. It is worth a visit.

There are many other buildings in Caen of equal interest. Top of the list is St. Nicholas'

The convent (Abbaye-aux-Dames), now St. Giles' Church, was founded by William's wife, Matilda, in atonement of their marriage ; they were distant cousins. It stands on a hilltop overlooking the harbour in Caen and its Romanesque architecture has remained purer than that of its contemporary, the Monastery.

Church, built by the monks of St. Stephen's as the church for a new urban district that took nine centuries to complete. It has without doubt one of the most beautiful and most typical Norman Romanesque naves in the area. Unfortunately, it is not open to the public and you can only see the exterior, after crossing the old romantic graveyard from which there is also an attractive view over the surrounding rooftops.

Saint-Michel de Vaucelles has a fine Romanesque tower, the remainder of the building dating from the 15th and 16th centuries.

Saint-Ouen still has a decidedly rustic air and seems to be more popular with poets than with archaeologists.

The surrounding area

Caen is an excellent centre from which to tour the surrounding area. We shall describe only two routes, the ones which seem to us to be the most characteristic.

The Orne Valley

A signposted ''tourist route'' leads through Louvigny and Feugerolles to the Coudray Bridge. From there, the road runs through Mutrecy to St-Laurent-de-Condel and on into the **Grimbosq Forest.** Purchased by Caen town council in 1972, the forest is open to the public and has been especially laid out for visitors. Leave your car on one of the car parks and enjoy the forest on foot. If you want to have a walk lasting a few hours, there are way-marked footpaths (cf. maps at exits to car parks). But if you prefer to rest for a while, have a look at the lake beyond the animal compound containing stags, deer, and wild boar. There are tables and benches all around the shores of the lake. Another point of departure is the ''Guillot Oak''. From there, you can try the trim course or follow the nature trail leading to an archaeological dig near the remains of an 11th-century manorhouse. Further on is St. Anne's Chapel, in a meander of the R. Orne ; its banks are also laid out as a picnic area.

Then drive on to **Thury-Harcourt.** At the entrance to the village, turn right and follow the road through the ''Roche à Bunel'', along a meander of the R. Orne. A few miles further on, is **Clécy**, the gateway to the Norman Alps. From here, you can choose between the banks of the R. Orne and more arduous travelling towards the summit of the ''Pan de sucre'' (Sugar loaf).

The beaches

The beaches are a major tourist attraction from Caen. Whatever the season, the trip has its own charm, on condition that you are kitted out to suit the weather !

A fast road leaving Caen from near the Convent takes you through **Hérouville** and on to Ouistreham. In Bénouville, take a short detour to **Ranville.** There, beside the bridge across the Caen Canal, there is a small museum that serves as a reminder of a combat during the Allied landings. On the night of 5th/6th June 1944, parachutists and gliders were sent here, bringing the British ''Pegasus'' Division that captured the bridge and protected the Eastern end of the front during the landings.

In **Ouistreham,** there is another museum, this time reminding visitors that it was here that the British troops landed at dawn on 6th June, preceded by a Free French commando. This resort is also famous for its beach and harbour, where large locks mark the end of the canal down to Caen harbour. Beyond the locks is the marina and the mouth of the R. Orne, an unspoilt area of marshland that is gradually being turned into an environmental and leisure centre.

Further along the coast to the west are the beaches of the Mother-of-Pearl Coast, in particular **Luc-sur-Mer,** which is famous for its iodine-filled air, and **Courseulles,** a small fishing harbour which has undergone a quite extraordinary level of development since the

The crypt in the Convent. The Romanesque crypt in the Convent contains a number of very fine capitals.

building of marinas and the expansion of its yacht harbour. Oyster parks provides visitors with a chance to taste fresh from the sea the shellfish that made the region prosperous during the last century.

After **Ver-sur-Mer,** we come to **Arromanches.** The concrete pontoons that protected the Mulberry harbour built by the Allies are still clearly visible. The various phases of the Allied landings are easy to understand after a visit to the very interesting Landing Museum (Musée du Débarquement). It is then an appropriate moment to pause and ponder in the vast American war cemetery above the beach at **Saint-Laurent-sur-Mer.** The road runs on through **Port-en-Bessin,** a bustling fishing harbour, and along to the **Pointe du Hoc,** an impressive cliff climbed by the commandos on 6th June 1944 in an attempt to capture guns... that were not there as expected.

On the way back, you will cross **Formigny,** the site of the last battle fought during the One Hundred Years' War. In **Bayeux,** you must stop and see the famous tapestry stitched by Queen Matilda, the "Tale of the Conquest" which describes the history of William's landing in England in 1066.

The face of Caen

The one thing that immediately strikes visitors is the uniformity of the building materials, the **wonderful white Caen limestone.** Every century since the 11th added some feature to the Monastery yet it remains a very homogeneous building. This stone, which was famous in years gone by, was used for all our historic buildings and was exported far afield, contributing to the town's fame but peppering the subsoil with galleries and huge chambers whose exact situation is not always known, thereby occasionally posing great problems on the surface, even at the present time. The architects involved in the rebuilding of Caen were fully aware of the advantages of this uniformity and all the buildings were faced with stone slabs which unfortunately had to be imported since the seams round Caen had petered out.

La Prairie, a rural area in the heart of the town, is only 700 yds. from the **St. Peter Basin,** strangling the town centre but serving as a reminder of its double vocation as an agricultural and maritime centre. Both types of activity were endangered in days gone by. La Prairie was saved from building by a decree signed in the Middle Ages giving the local people the right to harvest the second crop of grass. And now that the St. Peter Basin has been turned into a yachting marina, it too will be preserved, as a lake within the centre of the town.

Once the Folie-Couvrechef has been completed, Caen will have reached its territorial limits. Let us hope that its feverish thirst for expansion will then be quenched and that its continuing growth will show a regard for a virtue that seems to have characterised its history - **a sense of moderation.**

Nobody knows what the town will be like in the future, but let us remember what it was like in the past and learn from this experience ; history is a science that is becoming increasingly necessary. Caen is a changing town. Its prodigious expansion and the influx of new blood are putting it in danger of losing its own original character. As a "buffer" town between the rural areas of Lower Normandy and Paris, it must not forget that it is the capital of a region which is itself undergoing major development, but which still has a wealth of wonderful natural beauty spots.

Today, the outstanding feature of Caen is "the quality of life". Let us hope that the town maintains it so that it remains a town where life is sweet.

The Memorial museum : a museum for peace

One of the greatest battles in History took place in Normandy in 1944. Caen was the anvil of victory, the lynchpin in the encirclement of the 7th German Army. It was only right that this event should be inscribed in the local memory.

More than forty years have now passed. It is time for men of goodwill to be reconciled.

The apse in the Convent. The Romanesque apse of the Convent is particularly noteworthy for its four storeys.

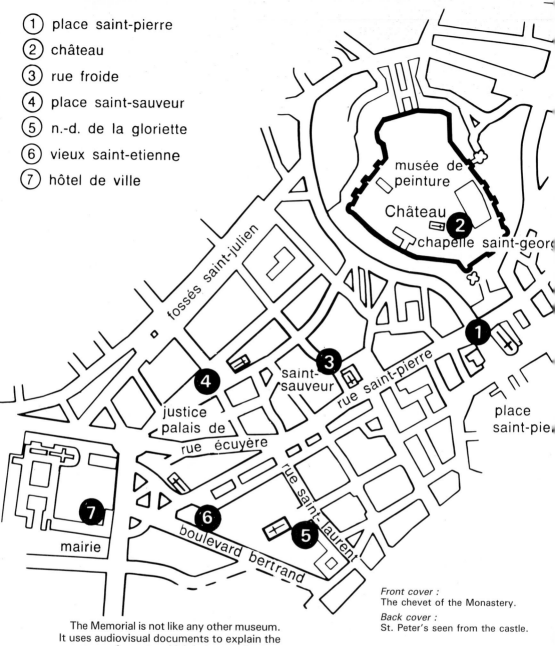

1. place saint-pierre
2. château
3. rue froide
4. place saint-sauveur
5. n.-d. de la gloriette
6. vieux saint-etienne
7. hôtel de ville

musée de peinture

Château

chapelle saint-georg

fossés saint-julien

saint-sauveur

rue saint-pierre

place saint-pie

justice palais de

rue écuyère

rue saint-laurent

mairie

boulevard bertrand

Front cover :
The chevet of the Monastery.

Back cover :
St. Peter's seen from the castle.

The Memorial is not like any other museum. It uses audiovisual documents to explain the sequence of events which led up to the outbreak of hostilities in 1939, the suffering of the European nations, the Allies' long period of preparation, the Landings, and the strategy behind the Battle of Normandy. It also highlights the fragility of our present-day freedom and the need for vigilance if we are to maintain it.

More than a mere page of history, the museum is a message from all who fell during this conflict, encouraging us to hold high the torch of liberty that they rekindled.

Memorial : Caen - La Folie-Couvrechef
Esplanade Général Eisenhower
Tel. 31 06 06 44
Open daily, 9.30 a.m. to 7.30 p.m. (10 p.m. in summer).

Estimated length of visit : 2 hours.

© 1989 EDITIONS OUEST-FRANCE - I.S.B.N 2.7373.0314.1 - Dépôt légal : mars 1989 - 1619.01.03.03.89
Imprimerie Raynard, La Guerche-de-Bretagne.